THE RETURN
of the
FOUR HOUR ROUND

Patrick Mateer

THE RETURN of the FOUR HOUR ROUND

Copyright © 2010 by Patrick Mateer

www.fourundergolf.com

Published by
Four Under Golf, LLC

ISBN 978-0-615-38177-0

Printed in USA

Design & Editorial Services by RB Images, Inc.
Cover Design and Illustrations By Roseanne Brown

TO DAD

You passed away in 1985, but every birdie
I make is still for you.

*"Son, always keep up with the group in front of you.
If you can't keep up, let the group behind play through."*

My first golf lesson, 1964.

PASSING ON THE VALUES OF THE GAME FROM GENERATION TO GENERATION

Mr. Mateer's book combines a sound message to all golfers with comic relief to accurately convey the current problem to the reader. My grandfather would always say, *"Golf is a game where you hit it, find it, and hit it again."* I believe that he is right, and THE RETURN of the FOUR HOUR ROUND is a truth that golfers need to embrace.

Connor Gall, *Portland, Oregon*
Son and Grandson

After the grip and the swing, the next thing my Dad taught me was how to keep up on the golf course. Maintaining a good pace isn't about skill level or hurrying. It's about doing a few simple things that keep the game flowing. Pat's book highlights the type of common sense solutions that my Dad taught me. If we all take the next step and pass it on to our fellow golfers, the four-hour round will again become a reality.

Chuck Gall, *Portland, Oregon*
Father and Son

When I began golfing 65 years ago, we could easily play 36 holes on any given day in well under eight hours. Now, it is difficult to finish one round some days, and 36 holes are almost impossible. This insanity has to stop. Golf is not much fun when you spend most of your day standing around and doing nothing. We have to get Pat's simple solutions out to the golfing public so we can once again enjoy golf as it's meant to be played – in four hours or less!

John Gall, *Pebble Beach, CA*
Grandfather and Father

CONTENTS

FOREWORD

Early Scottish golfers played at a brisk rate, walking quickly through wind and rain to hit the ball, finding it and hitting it again without wasting time. Somewhere between then and now we've lost our way to the point where the average round has slowed to a crawl. Not only has slow play turned golf into a much bigger investment in time than in the past, it has also taken a lot of enjoyment out of the game.

The reasons for slow play are many, with everything from ignorance to arrogance to blame – either people don't know any better, or they just don't care. Slow play is an epidemic that's incredibly frustrating, not only because it detracts from the game's enjoyment, but because although we can pinpoint its causes, no one has been able to formulate a simple, sensible, cohesive plan to fix it. Until now.

Pat Mateer is a long-time, authentic golfer (and friend) who understands the ins, outs and intricacies of the game better than just about anyone I've ever met. In this book, he's mapped out the many causes of slow play and identified the smart and simple ways to guarantee a four-hour round for any foursome.

When I was young and learning to play the game, golfers were taught to play fast – "*miss 'em quick*" was one of the first (and best) pieces of playing advice I received. I was also taught to be mindful of the group behind me and whether my group was slowing them down. (I'm amazed and appalled at how many golfers today move from the first tee to the 18th green without giving a single thought to how their pace of play affects all the players following them.)

I don't mean to imply that you have to rush your shots to maintain an agreeable pace. It's the time *between* swings that you have to learn to manage, and Pat is a master at explaining how. Just as important, he has rightfully recognized that to consistently play at a reasonable rate you have to develop a mindset in which you commit to responsible between-shot behavior. When you do, you'll most likely find that playing faster will help you develop a more effective pre-shot routine and a playing rhythm that results in lower scores. Could there be a better incentive?

Mark King, CEO and President
TaylorMade-adidas Golf Co.
March, 2010

INTRODUCTION

Do you ever get frustrated on the golf course waiting for the group in front of you to move out of the way? Do too many rounds seem to drag on forever? Are you spending more time on the course *watching-and-waiting* than actually *playing golf?* Are there times you want to walk up, tap someone on the shoulder and scream, *"For crying out loud, would you just hit it!"*

Enough is enough! I love golf as much as anyone, but my time is important to me. I'm tired of spending up to five hours on Saturday morning sitting on my golf bag or in my cart, watching the group in front lining up their putts like snails on Valium. It is not fun to play three holes only to arrive on the fourth tee and be greeted by one or two other groups still waiting to tee off. I hate having to make excuses to forego playing in member-guest tournaments because playing two or three 6-hour rounds is about as appealing as root canal surgery.

Whether you are good, bad, or average at the game, you are probably one of the millions of golfers around the world who feel the same way. We are the silent majority in the world of golf. We are the ones who sit in the clubhouse or grill room after the round scratching our heads or drowning our sorrows wondering why the round took so long, and why nobody does anything about it. We endure the frustration involved in hitting and waiting in the same vein as the rush hour commuter on his morning drive to work. Our dream is to play with a natural flow whereby our *golfing* is unimpeded. Unfortunately, this happens less and less as the years pass.

So, Mr., Miss, or Mrs. Golfer, what are we going to do about it? Write letters, complain to anyone that will listen, or run for Congress (I'm sure it would find a way to impose a tax)? If you are like most people, you have chosen to accept things the way they are, and continue on with your day-to-day life. You may choose to play less (as many have), or you may even quit the game (an unfortunate side effect of the problem).

The decisions we make about our recreational time have much to do with the joy we obtain from these activities. Slow play not only adds to the time required to play the game, it also diminishes the level of enjoyment. That's a deadly combination!

Can we really do something about ending slow play?

The answer is YES. It's not going to happen if we wait for others to solve the problem for us. If you are waiting for rulings and/or penalties to solve the problem, you will be waiting forever. If you think more marshals are the cure, you are mistaken. We have to quit waiting for others to solve this problem. The solution is in our hands.

So, get ready to kick-start the game along with millions of us who are fed-up with the menace of slow play. It's time to reclaim our game!

Welcome to Four Under Golf

SECTION ONE

GLOBAL SLOWING

Golf's Greatest Nemesis

JUST HIT IT!

THAT WHICH CONTINUALLY SLOWS WILL EVENTUALLY STOP

IS THIS WHERE WE ARE HEADED?

In the beginning, there was a club, a ball, and a hole in the distance. The golfer would hit the ball with his club until the ball finally came to rest in the hole. He then moved to the side of the completed hole, put his ball down and started hitting it toward the next hole. Golfers played either alone or in small groups. The process took about as long as it took to walk the distance of the holes played.

The years that followed brought millions of golfers into the game. What was once a few friends hitting a ball around a field became an international sport and an industry all its own. With the growing importance of competitions, the game became more serious. Television introduced more people to the game, and champion golfers became heroes to the multitudes. The game of golf boomed.

A side effect of this boom started to ease into the game during the latter part of the 20th Century. The game started to slow down. The 18-hole round that once took three hours to play moved past three-and-a-half hours to four hours.

Year after year it slowed, and four-and-a-half hour rounds became common. Near the end of the 20th Century, golfers were often taking over five hours to play. The beginning of the 21st Century introduced what was once unimaginable – the six-hour round!

Despite the best efforts of committees and governing bodies, nothing was able to stop the slowing of the game. People became frustrated and disenchanted. Every year it got slower, and slower, and slower.........

Is this the future of golf?

In the end, the game of golf finally came to a complete stop. The final match was a traditional event featuring the U.S. and European amateur champions. There were few golfers left in the world, as only a limited number could complete 18 holes in the same day. Golf courses had all but disappeared.

In the final match, the result was deemed a draw when play had to be stopped on the 12th green. The match was all-square at the time, and the gentlemen were moving at a rapid pace. They'd only been playing for 6 hours and 25 minutes. Then, without warning, the American champion completely froze in the middle of his putting stroke.

Everything seemed normal before this. He had successfully completed his standard seven-and-a-half minute routine. He counted the blades of grass on the 31-inch putt. He and his caddy surveyed the green from every angle, and calculated the break based on the slope, grain, and time of day. He knew there were 17 particles of sand spread randomly throughout his line, but being a champion, he'd seen tougher situations. After taking a mere 75 seconds to get the line on his ball pointing to the perfect position, he was ready to putt.

Then, all of a sudden as if lightning had struck, he froze! The putter was drawn back away from the ball exactly five-and-a-half inches. The slight left-to-right break appeared to be precisely calculated. But, there he was, frozen solid. His eyes didn't blink, and only through his breath was there any sign of life. He regained consciousness several hours later in the local hospital. It took doctors another two hours to pry the putter from his hands.

The doctors later termed it *'the frozen golfer syndrome'*. In any case, it was proclaimed that the game was far too dangerous for people to play, and all remaining golf courses were turned into city parks.

Years later, the chief surgeon who operated on the U.S. champion was asked about the cause of *'frozen golfer syndrome'*, and what could have been done to prevent it.

"The mind of the golfer finally overloaded. Much like too much voltage concentrated in one outlet can black out a circuit in your home, too much analysis finally froze our golfer. He had taken a simple act of moving a ball along the ground into a hole that was less than three feet away, and turned it into an operation more complex than brain surgery. A movement as simple as tossing an apple into a

trash container became a seven-and-a-half minute ordeal. Years of doing this finally froze him completely."

"How could this have been prevented?"

"The prevention is fairly straight forward. He should have learned to JUST HIT IT!"

---

*We'd hold our club and hit the ball,
and then we'd go and get it.*

*Now we stand and stare and fret
we forgot how to just hit it!*

WHAT SEEMS TO BE THE PROBLEM?

I am the problem.

And, you are the problem. We are the problem. That's the bad news. The good news is that since we are the problem, we can also be the solution. Now is the time to do something about it.

What is this problem that we are all currently part of? In the simplest of terms, it's slow play. We have taken golf from a flowing game resembling a leisurely drive in the country, to a stop-and-go activity resembling a freeway drive during rush hour. A game that can take two-and-a-half hours, is easily accomplished in three hours, is very pleasant at three-and-a-half hours, is acceptable at four hours, is beginning to crawl along at four-and-a-half hours, barely has a pulse at five hours, can now take up to six hours! All we are talking about is 18 holes of golf.

I wish I were kidding. A recent tournament I participated in featured a three-hour and 45-minute practice round, followed by a tournament round of five-hours and 52-minutes. If you think that's ridiculous, the group behind us was in the middle of the 17th fairway when we completed the 18th hole. They could not even keep up with the six-hour pace! You may be thinking that this was a corporate outing, or charity event with a group of beginners and part-time golfers. Wrong! This was a pro-scratch event with 50% professionals and 50% low handicap amateurs.

Playing golf at a slower pace each year has reached the point where the effects are more invasive. Researching this project introduced me to hundreds of articles, commentaries, and blogs on the subject. If you are interested in hearing what some of the truly frustrated, disillusioned, and angry golfers think about slow play, they are out there in full force. Here are a few samples of the mood:

"Slow play has become a universal curse in American golf and is talked about on every course in the country," says W. Eric Laing, author of <u>America! What Have You Done To The Auld Game?</u>

"Slow play in danger of killing the game," article by Karl MacGint – 2008.

Headlines in the *Golf Extra* section of the Feb. 11, 2010 Orange County Register: **Slow play not good for game at any level.** In Randy Youngman's article he notes – *"… the leaders made it only to the 15th hole before play was halted by darkness four hours and 24 minutes later. Aargh."* The article continues – *"It took (PGA Pro), who was in the final group on Sunday, so long to get through his pre-shot routine, on full shots and putts, I couldn't watch anymore."* And, finally – *"The problem with all of this slow play is that it rubs off on amateurs, many of whom now scrutinize*

*every putt from every angle and take
swings as (PGA Pro), leading to lor.
recreational rounds, especially on public cou*

Response to a 2007 blog: *"Personally, I find su
only the bane of golf, but also one of life's great , ,..eries.
In 20 years of playing competition golf, slow play is
undoubtedly the number one gripe of every player I've
played with. What I don't understand is if EVERYONE
complains about it, WHO is actually perpetrating the slow
play?"*

Here's one that got my attention: John White writes in one
of the blogs online, *"Slow play is the pimple on the ass of
golf. Everyone hates it, but they don't know how to get rid
of it."*

One of the more interesting perspectives I found on the
subject was in a book by Greg Rowley. <u>Golf, Naked</u> is a
book that I would describe as eclectic. It touches on most
every subject in the golfing world. Chapter 15 deals with
slow play in an insightful manner.

Like most of the articles I've read through the years, there
were some excellent points and ideas. He points out clearly
that *"It's important to understand that nothing can ruin a
golf experience like slow play. Nothing - bad weather,
lousy play, or idiot playing partners all pale in
comparison."*

What I found most relevant about Chapter 15 of <u>Golf,
Naked</u> was the first sentence in the final paragraph. *"If a*

of slow play persists, it might be time to consider changing your golfing habits." There, in a nutshell, is the key ingredient to the solution – changing our golfing habits.

Identifying these habits, explaining the far-reaching benefits of the correct set of habits, and the ramifications of the poor habits that have invaded the game, are the cornerstones for which the 4 Habits of the Four Under Golfer are based.

Here's one thing we all can see,
and it's time to admit it.

We'd play better and have more fun
if we'd get up and just hit it!

SHOULD WE BE WORRIED?

Have you been to a junior golf tournament lately? Do your kids play on a high school golf team? This is the next generation of golfers who will inherit the responsibility and leadership of our great game. What are we teaching these young people as we pass the torch?

I realize there are regions in the country (and the world) where issues are different, and circumstances vary. However, the following examples are certainly not isolated by any means.

A golf professional and good friend relates the following to me:

"My daughter is playing very well. She's the top junior in the region for her age, and broke 70 last week for the first time in a junior event."

"Wow, that's fabulous!" I exclaim. *"What's it like out there now? Do you get to watch her play in many events?"*

"It can be up to six hours to play. The other day she had to finish in the dark. It's HORRIBLE."

Recently, I played nine holes at a local course with three friends. We started on Hole #10 at 2:30 pm. At exactly the same time, the local high school team was teeing off on Hole

#1. They had six matches, with the final group teeing off at 3:20 pm.

My foursome finished our round and met on the patio overlooking the ninth green. We proceeded to chat and tell stories and lies about our round. We started to look at dinner menus. Peering out over the course, we watched as groups completed the ninth hole. At 6:05 pm. the final group exited the green, completing their nine holes in two hours and 45 minutes. Who won? It didn't appear that anyone cared too much. It looked like they were simply relieved to have lived through the ordeal!

Like many of you, I played junior golf and high school golf. I can say without reservation that if we had played a nine-hole high school match at the local golf club in more than two hours, we would not have been allowed to play that course again! It's sad, but true, but at my home club we inquire what time the high school team plays during the week because you DON'T want to get behind them. We knew it was a privilege to play at a golf club. Has it become a right?

We are spending unprecedented time, money, and resources teaching our children to swing the golf club. They learn to chip and putt with methods we never imagined. There are schools that can teach them about strength, nutrition, and mental attitude. The better young players today hit the ball further than the game had ever envisioned. My questions, however, are these: Who's teaching them about their responsibilities on the course?

Who's teaching them how to move around the golf course properly? Are they learning good habits, or bad habits?

We can't blame the next generation when we fail to teach, and live by, the basic values that are the foundation of the game. Great swings, long drives, and pure putts are a part of the golfer's quest. They are not, however, more important than the game itself. Losing sight of this is a dangerous path indeed.

The question heading this section is: Should we be worried? The answer: Only if we care about the future of the game.

The kids today go out and play
their talent has no limit.

The question now, have they learned how
to stand up and just hit it?

CHALLENGING OUR ROLE MODELS

Role models are important. Parents, grandparents, aunts, uncles, brothers and sisters have provided examples for our behaviors since the beginning of time. Others outside of the family also help to shape our behavior. People who influence us are often teachers, religious leaders, political figures, friends, business executives, athletes, coaches, and a host of others. Role models are individuals that we admire. We view their accomplishments as admirable. We often desire similar success for ourselves. To achieve this objective we mimic their behaviors.

The evolution of the game of golf is at a critical stage at the moment. We are in danger of succumbing to accepting the game as a slow and painstaking activity. Our choices are simple. 1) Accept the slowing. 2) Change our behaviors.

A key to changing our behaviors is to look closely at our role models. The largest contingents of our golfing role models are the professionals we view on television every week. Can we continue to accept all of their behaviors as "appropriate" because they are champion golfers?

We need to ask whether those we admire are taking us to golf's Promised Land, or to the Point-Of-No-Return. Consider the following:

The Masters is arguably the world's premier golf tournament. It is the only major championship played on the same golf course every year. The tournament is filled with tradition, and has produced countless memories for golfers of all generations. From Gene Sarazen's double – eagle in 1935 (*the shot heard around the world*), to Tiger's miraculous hole-out on #16 in 2005 (*the chip seen around the world*), the Masters is live theater at its finest.

A recent Masters featured a sincere effort on the part of the tournament committee to engage the viewing audience in a discussion about the state of the game. The Masters has always been a most charitable contributor towards the game, and an ardent supporter of its growth. Viewers were asked to forward suggestions as to: *"What can we do to grow the game of golf?"*

What was ironic about this was that anyone viewing the final round came face-to-face with a major problem affecting growth. The final twosome completed their 18-hole round in 5-hours and 10-minutes! *If it's going to grow, it can't be slow…*

Why would the length of time it takes two players to complete their round be a major issue? How does their round have any effect on you and me?

Here's how: Millions of golfers watch the Masters (and other televised golf events). We mimic what we see. We want to play like these great players. Bill, Tom, Sue, and

Sarah sit mesmerized to the screen watching the movements of their golfing idols. The following day, they are going out to play golf at their local club.

Do the math...

If it takes two people, shooting near par, 5-hours and 10-minutes to complete 18-holes of golf, how long is it going to take a foursome of golfers shooting between 80 and 95 to complete their round? After all, they just witnessed the behaviors of the greatest players. Certainly, if that's how they manage their way around the course it must be how we should play. The problem is that if we do this, a six-hour round will be considered *fast!*

Several years ago I was involved in various activities in the research of this project. One of the most amazing situations I came across was another example that points out that these incidents are, unfortunately, not isolated.

A sudden death playoff was required between two players who were tied for the lead after 72 holes. Both players were multiple champions in their own right. The first playoff hole was a par-3 measuring approximately 200 yards. The players drew for honors, and the sequence of events proceeded as follows:

Player A hit his tee shot on the green. He was approximately 25 feet from the hole.

Player B hit his tee shot into the right greenside bunker.

Player B had a good lie. He hit his bunker shot about 8 feet past the hole.

Player B marked his ball.

Player A hit his putt. It missed the hole, and he ended up 18 inches past the hole.

Player A marked his ball.

Player B missed his 8-foot putt. He tapped in for a bogey-4.

Player A made his 18-inch putt. Player A was deemed the winner.

The above scenario is certainly not an unusual sequence of events on a given par-3. Most golfers have played a par-3 hole with a playing partner in a similar manner. How long did it take these two players to manage this sequence of events (from the time the playing order was confirmed until the final putt dropped in the hole)?

Twenty-seven minutes! How long would it take to play a round of golf at that pace? *Do the math…*

Mimicking the actions of those we admire is a major part of the learning process in all sports. What pitcher in baseball didn't grow up trying to replicate the style of Sandy Koufax, Nolan Ryan, or Randy Johnson? Go to a little league game today and watch how many kids hold their hand up to the umpire in a manner resembling Derek Jeter. Whether they are runners, skiers, ballplayers, bowlers, or tennis players, we attempt to replicate the actions of those we admire.

Golf is a wonderful spectator sport. We, the golfing *participants* of the world, need to understand that we have a choice as to the behaviors we admire. Golfers at every level have behaviors that are beneficial to the game. However, even some of the greatest golfers in the world feature behaviors that should not be admired or replicated. We, the golfing spectators, must understand that our golfing idols are not always the greatest role models when it comes moving around the golf course. *"I'm sorry Mr. Professional - you're a great player, but I'm not going to stand there staring, waggling, contemplating, examining, and fumbling around like you. I'm going to play like Watson, Trevino, Palmer, Snead, Jones, and countless others who managed to shoot great scores and win tournaments without spending all day standing around contemplating the rotational spin of the planet. If you want me to watch you, cheer for you, and admire you, understand that I'm not alone out here. There are millions of golfers who are tired of the slowing."*

We can only hope that the mentors of the game will embrace Four Under Golf and once again display the positive behaviors that are beneficial to the game. If they don't, it's up to us to see right from wrong. It's up to us to do our part to stop the spread of global slowing!

It's true we learn from what we see
but this is what I've found.

That without change, forever lost
is the Four Hour Round.

ENTITLEMENT

THE MODERN EXCUSE FOR SLOW PLAY

A prevailing comment I hear from golfers who fall into the slow category is this: *"I paid my green fee, and I'll be damned if I'm going to rush around the golf course. I don't care if I'm holding people up. Let 'em wait!"* Ah, the joys of living in the age of entitlement.

Unfortunately, there are people who believe that their fee payments, or membership, or status, or even their ability, allows them to treat the golf course as their own personal entertainment center. This is comparable to a person driving in the fast lane on the freeway at 50 miles per hour, holding up a long line of frustrated drivers. *"I'm going fast enough, let them go around me if that's their desire."* Then, of course there are those who don't even look in their rear view mirror, and, frankly, could care less!

The rise in the concern for our rights, and our dependence on rules has diminished the value of responsibility as the guiding light for our behaviors. There is a more prevalent attitude of "because I can," as opposed to "because I should" in modern culture. You don't have to look too hard to observe this. Unfortunately, this attitude has crept into golf.

Just what is the golfer entitled to when he or she pays the green fee? Does this mean he can wander around the course like a lost puppy? Does this entitle her to play in six hours with a 30-minute lunch break? Is it OK for his buddy to give him five-minute golf lessons before each shot?

The golfer's entitlement is this: You have either paid money, or somehow managed to be welcomed onto the golf course. This entitles you to play the course. Your OBLIGATION, regardless of how you manage to get to the first tee, is to keep pace with the field or move aside and let others pass. When you begin a round of golf, this is your responsibility regardless of your ability or status.

You've paid your fee; you're on the tee
in less than 15 minutes.

You've agreed today, despite your pay
to keep up and just hit it!

"THE SURVEY SAYS...."

This project started with a simple survey distributed to a wide variety of golfers. This included golf professionals, top amateurs, average golfers and high handicappers. It also included men and women, young and old. There was a balanced selection of private club members and public course players. The objective was to find out how people felt about the current pace of play in golf.

The results of the survey proved revealing to say the least.

Question 1: Slow play in golf is:

A MAJOR Problem	32%
A problem	43%
A nuisance	23%
Not a problem	2%
Golf is played too fast	0%

Question 2: I consider myself:

A very fast player	21%
A faster than average player	50%
An average player	27%
A slower than average player	2%
A very slow player	0%

Question 3: My ideal 18-hole round of golf in a foursome takes:

3 hours or less	3%
3 ½ hours	65%
4 hours	32%
4 ½ hours	0%
5 hours or more	0%

Question 4: Tournament golf, relative to normal golf is:

Much slower	77%
A little slower	17%
About the same	6%
Faster	0%

Question 5: In tournament golf, slow play:

I hate it, and sometimes choose not to play	29%
I don't like it, and it often upsets me	56%
It is slow, but it's OK with me	6%
It is fine with me	7%
I enjoy the slower pace	2%
It's too fast for my liking	0%

Question 6: If the pace of golf improved:

Golfers would play better	68%
Golfers would play about the same	32%
Golfers would play worse	0%

Question 7: If the pace of golf improved:

Golfers would enjoy it more	88%
Golfers would enjoy it about the same	12%
Golfers would enjoy it less	0%

Question 8: If the pace of golf improved:

More golfers would play; fewer would quit playing	72%
About the same amount would play	28%
Fewer golfers would take up the game	0%

Analyzing these results leads us to some interesting conclusions. It also reveals some of the challenges that the game has had in dealing with the growth of slow play through the years.

Conclusion 1: Slow play is a problem. There is a range of emotions when it comes to the subject of slow play. What is obvious is that more than 70% of golfers feel that slow play is a problem. In fact, one out of every three golfers believes that slow play is a MAJOR problem.

Even those who don't feel it's a major threat to the game of golf generally feel it's a nuisance. When you have less than 5% of the golfers stating that it's not an issue at all, and NOBODY feeling that golf is played too fast, this is an area of the game that certainly needs to be addressed.

Conclusion 2: Tournament golf is VERY slow. When nearly 30% of golfers HATE the pace of play in golf tournaments to the extent where they consider nonparticipation, we have a real problem. Less than 20% of the golfers feel the pace is "OK" If you are in this group, it's time you understand that more than 80% of us are far from happy about it!

Conclusion 3: Golfers enjoy playing in four hours and under. And, their enjoyment diminishes as the length of time increases. They also believe that if golf was played at four hours and under: A) we'd play better, B) we'd enjoy playing the game more, and C) more people would gravitate to the game.

Conclusion 4: The game of golf is played too slowly, but apparently there are no slow golfers! BINGO... This is a major issue that needs to be dealt with. Like so many areas of our lives, if we want to understand and solve a problem – we should first look in the mirror! There were golfers involved in this survey who couldn't play 18 holes in less than four hours playing alone, with a golf cart, and two fore-caddies, yet "none of them" were slow players!

In a nationwide survey conducted by a major golf publication, the questions were asked:

1) How would you rate your pace of play?

Fast	57.8%
Average	37.4%
Slow	4.8%

2) How would you rate other golfer's pace of play?

Slow	56.2%
Average	41.8%
Fast	2.0%

So, somewhere between 2% and 60% of us are fast players, about 40% are average, and somewhere between 5% and 60% are slow players. Denial is running rampant in the golfing world! It's time for thousands of golfers to wake up, look in the mirror, and say, *"Hi, I'm _____ and I'm a slow player."* Trust me, you're not alone, and there is help. Read on!

Slow play is generally perceived as someone else's problem. Here is a personal story highlighting this:

Several years ago I was involved in a golf event in Puerto Vallarta, Mexico. After the opening round, a participant approached me and gave me the standard play-is-too-slow lecture. He couldn't understand why a two-man scramble took more than five hours to play. He was passionate and sincere, and I could relate to his frustration.

The following day featured a better-ball event. The course was not crowded this day, and my partner and I joined up with another group. It was a shotgun start, and the four of us started on tee #1. The group ahead of us started on tee #7. We had six open holes in front of us.

We had played about seven holes when a member of our foursome announced: *"This is awesome. If golf was played at this pace every day, I'd start playing more golf again."* We caught the group on the 13th tee. We had completed 12 holes, and they were playing their seventh hole. They were also two holes behind the group in front of them. And, of course, the gentleman who lectured me the day before was part of the group we'd just caught! Needless to say, the gentleman in our group quickly remembered why he didn't play as much golf anymore.

A more recent story truly brings to light the issue of self-awareness when it comes to pace of play.

My dentist is a good friend of mine. We had only played together once, but Mel was a slow player. He was like the guy at your club that people whisper about. *"Have you ever played with Mel? Well, be prepared for a long day."*

I had a group of six golfing buddies at the house for a barbeque, and I gave Mel an early draft of <u>THE RETURN of the FOUR UNDER ROUND</u>. I wanted his comments, and noted that I gave this to him because he was a slow player. To this he said, *"Am I really? You're the first person that's ever told me that."* The response brought shock, stares, and finally laughter from the others at the table. In more than 25 years of playing golf, NOBODY had said a word to Mel about his pace of play.

I'm pleased to say that Mel's review of the draft not only awakened his senses; it also assisted in the completion of the final version you are currently reading. Understanding that slow players DON'T REALIZE that they are slow is an important factor in solving this problem. The fact that slow players are seldom informed or confronted about their pace-of-play is an essential element to consider.

How did Mel play after reading the original <u>THE RETURN of the FOUR UNDER ROUND</u> draft? Ten days following completion he shot his lifetime low round of 78 on his home course. *"It was great. I played like I always knew I could. I simplified everything, got up and just hit it! It was the most liberating feeling I've ever had on the golf course."*

Four Under Golf deals with pace-of-play on a personal level. We must accept that pace of play is an issue we are all involved in. We need to confront, and be confronted. Each of us should first look into the mirror. And finally, we need to learn (or re-learn) what it takes to play Four Under Golf. The 4 Habits of the Four Under Golfer are designed to give ALL golfers the simple tools required to play the game of golf as it was intended.

---

*The game's too slow, and it won't grow
if we don't wake up and get it.*

*It starts with me, and now I see
the way is to just hit it!*

THE RETURN of the FOUR HOUR ROUND

THE TIME IS NOW!

I spoke to a woman recently about <u>THE RETURN of the FOUR UNDER ROUND</u>. She is an avid golfer and I knew she would be interested in the subject. The first words out of her mouth portrayed a thoughtful question. *"What are you going to do about the people in front of me?"*

This is a woman who loves golf. She HATES slow play to the point where she now rarely plays. *"I simply can't stand five and six hour rounds!"* Her question was valid, to say the least. Here is a woman who plays golf at a responsible pace. Now, she has virtually quit the game. Meanwhile, golfers who wander around the course like lost sheep are everywhere.

There was a time when the dysfunctional golfer was taken aside and taught how to move around the golf course. Today, the functional golfer is left with few choices. These choices go from bad to worse:

1) *Continue to play in the same manner*. When there are few players on the course, we rejoice. When play is plentiful, we simply sit and wait between shots and deal with the frustration.

2) *Start playing in a dysfunctional manner.* We change our behaviors to match those of golfers taking endless amounts of time to play the game.

3) *Quit playing.* We can't take it anymore!

The slow players are currently winning the battle for control of the game of golf. Instead of the slow player altering his or her behavior, the golfer who plays at an acceptable pace is forced to slow down. In too many cases, the functional golfer becomes dysfunctional. This must not continue!

The following section outlines the solutions to global slowing. What is important to understand is that we CANNOT SURRENDER. Golfers have been slowing down, altering good behaviors, and quitting the game for too long. It's time for this to change.

Enough is enough...

Even though the golf is slow
our behaviors must stay sound.

For the time is now for the return
of the Four Hour Round.

SECTION TWO

SHIFTING GEARS

Reversing the Slowing Trend
Once and For All

THE 4 HABITS
OF THE FOUR UNDER GOLFER

Introducing: FourUnder Fred

Hi, I'm FourUnder Fred. *I'm going to do my best to pass on the habits that my father, ThreeUnder Ted, taught me when I first started playing golf. Believe me, if I can learn these habits, you can too. I guarantee that once these habits become part of your golfing life, you'll have more fun and play much better. Plus, you'll be more enjoyable to play with!*

I'm grateful to my dad for introducing me to golf. The game grew and prospered because he did his part in passing on a better game to my generation. Now, it's my job to do my part.

Let's get started...

The pace of play at which the game of golf is played has been slowing for many years now. Nobody wanted this to happen. It wasn't some master plan to make the game less enjoyable. It is, however, the manner in which the game has evolved.

We need to halt this slowing trend, and usher in THE RETURN of the FOUR UNDER ROUND! The alternative is not attractive: Longer rounds of golf at a slower pace, less enjoyment, more golfers leaving the game, diminishing viewership, and a decline in THE GAME. We are already seeing these trends.

What has to change in order to reverse the slowing trend? The answer – the behaviors we display during each round of golf... our habits!

Here's a simple question to take to the golf course that will open your eyes:

You are playing with Tom, Bill, and Joe in a foursome. Tom is putting. What are you doing?

This question relates to the heart of the 4 Habits of the Four Under Golfer. There are numerous scenarios, and they all have different answers. Have you already putted out? Are you putting next? Are you third in line to putt? Where is your ball in relation to Tom's?

Each of the possible scenarios has answers that define your particular golfing habits. Are you prepared? Are you in position? Are you ready to move with purpose? What are your next movements?

Read on, and the importance of the simple question – "What am I doing now?" will become crystal clear. We all have responsibilities during the course of a round of golf, and they go way beyond the few minutes during a round that we are actually swinging the club.

The 4 Habits of the Four Under Golfer are nothing more than good habits that need to replace the bad habits many golfers exhibit. A habit reflects learned behaviors that we have repeated over time.

In the game of golf, we all establish behavior patterns from the time we begin playing. We are taught how to grip the club, how to stand up to the ball, and how to swing. We repeat activities during this process to the point where they are habitually part of our game. Without this ability, every time we played the game would resemble starting over.

We also learn how to move around the golf course. There are two distinct activities we are involved in during a round of golf: 1) swinging the golf club and hitting the ball, and 2) playing golf and moving around the course. Combining these activities gives us GOLF. Nearly 100% of all the teaching and learning involving the game of golf is centered on #1 above. Teaching golfers to play golf and move responsibly around the golf course is sadly neglected.

So, the modern golfer learns how to swing the golf club, but is left alone to decipher how to move around the course. *"OK, Bill, you've now got a swing working, and you know some of the rules – get out there and play. You'll figure the rest out while you're out there."*

Golfers don't play slow because they want to. They simply have developed a series of poor habits that make it challenging for them to move around the golf course in a functional manner. In other words, they don't know HOW TO play golf at an acceptable pace because the behaviors they've developed on the course make it difficult to impossible.

The assumption that moving around a golf course is a natural act and no teaching is required – IS A FALLACY!

There is only one way to rectify this situation, and that's to instill habits in each of us that are beneficial to our game, and THE GAME.

THE 4 HABITS
OF THE FOUR UNDER GOLFER

1) BE PREPARED
2) BE IN POSITION
3) MOVE WITH PURPOSE
4) SIMPLIFY YOUR ROUTINES

THE 4 HABITS

1.) Be Prepared
2.) Be in Position
3.) Move with Purpose
4.) Simplify your Routines

That's it!

Moving around the course is not about hurrying or rushing. Playing at a better pace doesn't diminish any of the great experiences of our game. It adds to them!

Four Under Golf is not about taking away from any of the joy that our time on the golf course gives to us. It is about minimizing the *wasted time*.

I've got no clue what I should do
and it's time that I admit it.

I've got bad habits that need to change
so I, too, can just hit it!

HABIT #1
BE PREPARED

My dad's favorite coach was so incredible, he was universally known as "the wizard". Coach John Wooden won more NCAA basketball championships than any coach, and he started his first practice each year the same way – teaching players to tie their shoes. He understood that the foundation for success was preparation, and it started from the ground up.

"Fail to Prepare, and Prepare to Fail"

Being prepared is essential in all successful ventures. Playing golf is no different.

Here's the checklist I adhere to prior to each round.

1) Mark my ball for identification.
2) Have tees in my pocket.
3) Have a second ball marked, and in my pocket.
4) Make sure all my clubs are accounted for.
5) I have a scorecard and a pencil.
6) Do I need an umbrella?
7) Do I have a rain jacket and pants?
8) Do I have plenty of golf balls?

I know my starting time, and make sure I'm on the first tee well in advance. The entire flow of a golf course begins with players adhering to this responsibility. Delaying the first tee process has a ripple effect for everyone on the course.

Once you've begun your round, being prepared to hit each and every shot without slowing down your group, and the entire field of golfers behind you, is YOUR responsibility. The more you are prepared, the easier this becomes.

Each action we take during a round of golf requires preparation. Far too often, golf has become a game where the first player hits his shot, followed by everyone moving to the second player's ball. This same process continues as the group moves around the course. This is a recipe for disaster.

When we play golf, we are participants, not spectators. We are not at home watching golf on television; we are on the course PARTICIPATING. It's fine to observe the other players in your group as they hit their shots, but this should not take the focus away from your preparation.

Remember to be prepared when it's your turn to hit, and you will find the game far more rewarding.

You're on the tee, with Jim and Lee
who've waited for five minutes.

While you look for tees and balls and gloves,
it's your turn to just hit it!

FourUnder Fred's
KEYS TO PREPARATION

1) <u>BE PREPARED</u>

2) BE IN POSITION

3) MOVE WITH PURPOSE

4) SIMPLIFY YOUR ROUTINES

1) **Think ahead.** What's my next shot going to be? What clubs should I take with me in order to play the shot(s) ahead of me? What else do I need (towel, extra ball, extra clubs)?

2) **Know where everything is.** We should all know what we have in our golf bags, and where each item is located. Being prepared helps eliminate wasted time.

3) **Preparation doesn't stop while others play.** You don't need to wait for all action to stop in order to prepare. This includes: Putting clubs away, picking up your spare clubs, towels, umbrellas and other assorted items, writing down scores, lining up your putt, repairing divots, and a host of activities that are part of being a participant in the game.

THE UNPREPARED GOLFER

1) He's the one writing down scores when it's his turn to tee off.

2) She's the one walking to the cart to get her putter following her bunker shot.

3) He's the one walking back to the cart to get another club because he only brought one with him and decided to change.

4) He's the one on the green who watches Bill putt, then asks the group *"Am I away?"*

5) She's the one that is never ready when it's her turn.

HABIT #2
BE IN POSITION

I'm a baseball fan. Like all sports, baseball has a flow to it. This flow exists because everyone knows where he or she is supposed to be, and when he or she is supposed to be there.

Think of the sequence of events in golf relative to a baseball team coming to bat. The batter is up to the plate attempting to hit the ball being thrown by the pitcher. The player who is coming to bat next is waiting in the on-deck circle. He has his helmet on, his bat in hand, and he is watching the pitcher in preparation for his turn to bat. The player in the hole is in the dugout with his helmet and his bat, ready to move into the on-deck circle.

Imagine the flow of a baseball game if Derek Jeter got a hit, then Alex Rodriguez had to get off the bench, find his bat, put on his helmet, walk out of the dugout, take a bunch of swings, then step into the batter's box. That would be a very time-consuming, ineffective, and wasteful way to play baseball, wouldn't it? Unfortunately, that's how golf is played by FAR TOO MANY golfers.

The flow of golf depends on golfers understanding the concept of properly positioning themselves during the round. The fact that golfers no longer learn this is a major contributor to the slowing of the game. Without this flow, it's going to be slow!

Here is my standing mantra:

"Find your on-deck circle, and move into it prepared to play!"

Create a thought pattern that is fun and effective. *"OK, Bill is preparing to play, and it is my shot next. Where am I going to position myself that is going to allow me to get to my ball in the most efficient manner without disturbing Bill?"* Then, position yourself there!

Being in position also involves positioning your equipment. This includes your golf bag, cart, and items carried with you from shot to shot. These items need to always be placed: A) in clear sight, B) in a position which allows them to be retrieved along the path to your next destination, and C) in a location which does not effect play. Your movements should always be as straight-line as possible.

THE RETURN of the FOUR HOUR ROUND

There is always a correct area to position yourself and your equipment during a round of golf. This requires no rushing. It only requires awareness. It comes with the distinct understanding that you are a participant in the game, and not simply a spectator. Developing this simple habit will help you on your way to becoming a Four Under Golfer!

Bill is hittin' and Tom is sittin'
and they don't seem to get it.
There's a place to keep the pace,
to stand before you hit it!

FourUnder Fred's
KEYS TO BEING IN POSITION

1) BE PREPARED

2) **BE IN POSITION**

3) MOVE WITH PURPOSE

4) SIMPLIFY YOUR ROUTINES

1) **Find your On-Deck Circle:** Know when you're next in line to hit, and find that spot that allows you to move directly to your ball without hindering the play of others.

2) **You are a participant**: Watching others play is part of the enjoyment of the game. Learn to do this while at the same time placing yourself in position to play without delay. The guy in the on-deck circle certainly observes, but he is READY when it's his turn.

3) **Understand where you're going next**: If you've completed a hole, or a shot, locate your next destination and place yourself, and your equipment, in position to move there without delaying play. Know where the next tee

is. Know where your bag/cart is located. Be aware of how your movements affect play.

THE OUT-OF-POSITION GOLFER

1) He positions himself where he has the best view, with no regard to his next role as a participant.

2) She treats each shot in golf as a separate entity, and when it's her turn, she'll move to her ball. She pays little or no attention to her location beforehand.

3) He sits in the cart until his playing partners remind him – *"It's your turn to play!"*

HABIT #3
MOVE WITH PURPOSE

When I was younger, the *Under* family would always watch Seinfeld together. There was a classic episode where Kramer creates a coffee table book about coffee tables. Well, Four Under Golf can be looked at in a similar manner.

It's a movement about movement!

A round of golf requires an assortment of movements. How we manage these affects the entire game. Look at me. I'm short and squat with tiny legs. Is there a new class that golfers take to teach them to move in slow motion? I play with golfers twice my size that I move past while giving them a 20-yard head start.

Playing golf is not like running a 50-yard dash, or swimming the 500-meter freestyle, but my goodness, it's not meant to be a picnic, or slow-motion stroll in the park!

If you are not a quick mover, plan your movements. It's OK to stand on the edge of the green nearest your cart or bag as the group finishes putting. It's fine to be sitting in your cart, or near your golf bag when the last player in your group tees off. However, if you're of normal physical conditioning, there is no reason for you to meander around the golf course like someone 30 years your senior.

To move with purpose, you must understand your purpose. Your purpose is to move to your next shot/position in an effective and efficient manner. Managing this properly is one of the primary responsibilities we all share.

We can argue whether it's an athletic endeavor, but golfers must admit it.

We may not run, but we have more fun when we move and then just hit it!

FourUnder Fred's
KEYS TO MOVING WITH PURPOSE

1) BE PREPARED

2) BE IN POSITION

3) <u>MOVE WITH PURPOSE</u>

4) SIMPLIFY YOUR ROUTINES

1) **The shortest distance between two points is a straight line:** Don't meander around the course like a lost puppy. We can walk up the fairway together, but when it's time to separate, we need to move toward our ball. Moving in packs from shot to shot is unacceptable.

2) **Think ahead:** If you are sharing a cart with Bill, it's fine to leave him and move to your ball while he is preparing his shot. Either you take the cart yourself, or walk towards your ball – AND remember to bring your clubs with you!

THE WANDERING GOLFER

1) This is the golfer who appears to be lost. He's the one whose journey from tee to green resembles someone driving from Los Angeles to Chicago – via Seattle!

2) He's the guy who tees off last, then goes to the drinking fountain on his way to his bag. Following this he writes down the scores from the previous hole then runs back to the tee where he forgot his towel.

3) She's the golfer who helps Mary look for her ball in the right rough area, and then walks backward to her ball on the other side of the fairway to play her shot.

COMBINING THE FIRST 3 HABITS

BE PREPARED ➡ BE IN POSITION ➡ MOVE WITH PURPOSE

Departing the green is the perfect test of our first three golfing habits.

The group that includes prepared and positioned golfers moving with purpose:

When the final player's putt goes into the hole, a playing partner replaces the pin. The remaining players are positioned in an area that is closest to their carts/bags (but able to still view the final player's putt). All players have their extra items (clubs, towels, etc...) with them. The final player to putt-out has his extra items in a position in direct line to his cart/bag. This limits the opportunity for lost items, and expedites departure. After the pin is replaced,

---

the entire group departs the green without delay. This allows the group behind immediate access to the green.

The group that includes the poorly positioned wanderers of the links:

When the final player's putt goes into the hole it often resembles the conclusion of *SixOver Sam's* birthday party (my nephew). There are kids moving around everywhere. Everyone's looking for their toys, and there is no rhyme or reason where they might be.

When Tom finishes putting in this group, it's the adult version of the same scene. Nobody has picked up the pin, so Tom has to get the pin and replace it. Then, of course, the wedge he chipped with is on the other side of the green. Bill is standing in the middle of the green counting his shots. Joan is walking to the back of the green, and Bill has to tell her *"can you get the cart for us, please?"* – So, she has to go back to the front of the green where they left it (wrong position, of course). And, then there's Herbert. He's hitting his 20-foot putt again while the group behind is waiting to hit. When Herbert finally walks off the green, he's moving as slow as humanly possible for a 30-year old man.

Watching people depart greens and tees will reveal a lot about the functional or dysfunctional habits of your fellow golfers.

HABIT # 4
SIMPLIFY YOUR ROUTINES

Watching Kobe Bryant play basketball the other night, I marveled at how he took just one dribble and shot those free throws into the basket time after time. Do you think he'd do better if his routine took 30 or 40 seconds? How about a minute or more?

ThreeUnder Ted once told me, *"Son, focus on your target and hit the ball. Standing there and thinking about it for too long isn't going to do you any good. There's a big difference between taking your time and wasting your time. If you want to be a golfer, you need to learn the difference."*

What are your routines? Here's a list of activities for which golfers generally adapt a routine. You may have some additional ones that you employ during a round:

1) Teeing up your ball.

2) Lining up your shot.

3) Practice swings, waggles, deep breaths, etc…

4) Getting yardages.

5) Post-shot activities.

6) Lining up putts.

7) Standing over your shot.

The above constitutes a partial list of activities that are (or are not) a part of a golfer's routines.

The time utilized to perform these actions can vary from a few seconds to several minutes. Your responsibility as a golfer is to simplify your routines to the point where you are able to play the game at an acceptable pace (four hours and under).

Today's professionals that we watch on television each week are often great role models to golfers in many ways.

Unfortunately, the routines that many of these ladies and gentlemen have developed are NOT good models for us to follow. We must realize that they are, in fact, entertainers as well as golfers. Admire their swings, marvel at their shots, but view their "antics" as theater.

Here are a few examples:

The post-shot-stand-and-stare – This has become the expected response to virtually every shot that does not end up in the perfect location. It is often accompanied by a conversation with the caddy, hands held outstretched with a gaze into the heavens, maybe a couple of practice swings, and a general look of disbelief before finally moving on. Variations on this theme travel from the tee shot through to the shortest of putts. Now, of course, the golfers of the world have adopted this non-beneficial behavior into their repertoire of poor habits, doing nothing but adding to the slowing of the game.

I'm getting all the information, and I'm going to do it slowly – A famous golf pro once told *ThreeUnder Ted* that he picked his clubs as follows: *"I'd look at the shot, figure what club would put me just over the green, and then I'd hit one less."* That was, of course, before the days of yardage markers and range finders.

The entire slowing of the game and the reliance on information as our guide to playing golf is misguided at best. Information is vital, of course. However, its position of perceived importance has elevated well out of proportion. Combining this with the time spent obtaining this "information" once again adds to our global slowing.

Remember this – the goal is to gather enough information to steer toward the target and away from danger. Relying excessively on information takes instinct away as a guiding force and becomes a detriment to our growth as golfers.

Peyton Manning drops back to pass. It's 32 degrees, and the wind is blowing 20 miles per hour. There are 75,000 screaming fans in the stadium, and millions watching on television. Within seconds, he passes the ball 25 yards to his receiver running full speed over the middle. The pass hits the receiver in full stride, as two defenders miss the ball by less than six inches each. He had information. He FELT the wind. He had a PREPARED play. His players were in POSITION. Everyone moved with PURPOSE. His ROUTINE was SIMPLE and effective. His pass, however, was a reflection of a competitor PLAYING the game.

"This pass was important," notes the commentator. Would it have benefited or hindered Manning if he had much more time to: check the wind speed and direction (throw some grass into the air), take some practice throws, discuss the route in detail with his receiver, check the firmness of the turf, get the crowd to quiet down, chat about the snap of the ball with his center, get all the blockers perfectly lined up, and finally – lining up the seams of the ball perfectly for maximum rotational spin? I'll let you answer that question.

Remember – golf is a sport requiring instinct and movement. If you want to spend several hours *thinking* your way to success, take up the game of chess.

When you learn to simplify your routines, and allow yourself to *play* the game, you'll reap the following rewards:

1) You will play better.

2) You will enjoy the game more.

3) You will be more enjoyable to play with.

4) You will play at a better pace.

5) We ALL will play at a better pace.

Simplifying your routines is going to help you on every level. All you need to do is practice and institute the changes. You'll improve your game, add to your enjoyment, and help improve THE GAME!

We've all seen the pre-shot routine
it seems you can't forget it.

Not to be mean, but you want to scream:
"is he ever going to hit it?"

FourUnder Fred's
KEYS TO SIMPLIFYING YOUR ROUTINES

1) BE PREPARED
2) BE IN POSITION
3) MOVE WITH PURPOSE
4) <u>SIMPLIFY YOUR ROUTINES</u>

1) **Think "free throws":** It is important to understand that having simple and effective routines will improve your game. Overextending the time put into the preparation of each shot will have no positive effects on your performance. Prepare, and then trust your instincts.

2) **Plan early:** Make Habit #1 a part of your game, and this will help you with your routines. If you are prepared to play when it's your turn, your routines will simplify.

3) **Watch TV with caution:** There are players we watch on television that should have a sign posted on them – "Don't try this at home."

We must realize:

A) Just because they are on television doesn't mean their habits are healthy for our game.

B) There are some televised golfers with habits worth following. The problem is that since they don't take up as much time in front of the camera (fiddling around), their "routines" do not become images we remember. The result is that we mimic behaviors detrimental to the game, while the positive behavioral examples go unnoticed.

This needs to change!

THE FAR-FROM-SIMPLE ROUTINE GOLFER

1) The multiple practice swinger: I never take a practice swing. I figure I'm going to take enough swings during the round! Have you ever seen a quarterback in the huddle practice throwing? If you need practice swings to feel your rhythm, that's fine, one is plenty.

2) The "look-at-it-from-all-sides" putter: What percentage of golfers do you think do this because they saw it on TV? My personal favorite is the guy who goes to the side of the putt, some 20 feet from nowhere, and gets down in a crouched position. *"Dave, you're a 14 handicap and you haven't made a 20-foot putt in six months – what are you doing?"*

3) The yardage fanatic: This is the guy who goes through his yardage check and comes up with the fact he's 242 yards from the pin. He can only hit the ball 195, but still spent 90 seconds getting the *"exact"* yardage even though he could see the 200-yard marker in the distance. The "yardage fanatics" are EVERYWHERE!

YOUR FRIENDLY OPTION
"LET 'EM PLAY THROUGH"

A mandatory behavior in the golfing world should ALWAYS be: *"If the group behind you is playing faster than you, let 'em play through."* It's as simple as that.

Here are a few misconstrued scenarios:

1) *"We're playing at a four-hour pace, we don't need to let anyone play through."*

This is an absurd argument. There is no maximum speed limit on a golf course. If you're driving your car 65 mph on a highway with no speed limit, and a car approaches from behind at 100 mph, you move over and let them pass. The same applies here.

2) *"We'll let them through on the next par-3."* This is all well and good if the par-3 hole is coming up shortly. However, there is nothing wrong with moving aside on any hole to let faster players play through.

3) *"We were going to let them pass on the par-3, but when we got to the green, they weren't ready to hit."* If you've

been holding them up, you can put the flag back in the hole and let them pass.

There is an art to letting players pass through. It is important to understand, because no matter how you play, you will be in that situation at some time. The key is to continue to move forward with your own game during the process. By this I mean:

A) If you wave a group up to the green on a par-3 hole, move aside while they hit. After they hit their tee shots, it is acceptable for players in your group to putt while the group approaches the green. When they arrive at the green, cease your activities and allow them to continue.

B) If you are waiting on a tee to let a group pass through, go ahead and hit your tee shots before the group arrives. Following this, allow them to hit, and then feel free to move up the fairway while this group plays ahead.

The key to letting golfers play through is to allow them to pass without your group falling further behind.

Remember, it is not a sign of weakness to allow another group to play through. It is a sign of courtesy. It shows respect for your fellow golfers. This aspect of the game needs to return as practice followed by golfers worldwide.

*Play on through, we ask of you
then we don't have to sweat it.*

*We won't hurry and you won't worry
be our guests to just hit it!*

THE 10-SECOND SOLUTION

It's about time! It's about time we did something about slow play. And – it's about time – YOUR time! How do we impress upon fellow golfers that it's simple to improve the pace-of-play? It's not difficult at all.

The 10-second solution is a simple concept, with far reaching benefits.

A foursome of golfers shoots 78, 80, 82, and 85. They play in five hours. What do they have to alter in order to play in four hours? Answer: Take 10 fewer seconds to hit each shot. That's it! This includes time spent: getting to the ball, pre-shot routine, getting yardages, throwing grass to check wind, departing the green, lining up shots, raking traps, and the host of other activities that make up "playing" a round of golf.

Count to 10........... It's not very long, is it? Now, check yourself the next time you play. Watch your fellow golfers. Notice the group in front of you that you've been waiting on all day. You'll understand that slow play is about "wasted" time. That's time that is non-productive, and detrimental to the game on all levels.

Ten seconds is not a lot of time
and we all have to admit it.

We can all improve the way we move
before we have to hit it!

EMBRACING THE 4 HABITS
OF THE FOUR UNDER GOLFER

Learning and implementing each of the 4 Habits are the fundamental responsibilities of every golfer. Global slowing will only end when we teach, learn, and embrace these behaviors. If we can teach and expect golfers to play without stepping in the putting line of other golfers (even though the effect is negligible at most), then the 4 Habits need to become MANDATORY behaviors. After all, while stepping in another player's line is poor etiquette, playing golf without embracing the 4 Habits is negatively affecting the very essence of the game.

The Four Under Golfer plays golf utilizing the 4 Habits. Or, another way of putting this – The Four Under Golfer plays GOLF!

THE FOUR UNDER GOLFER

When It's My Turn To Play .... I'm Prepared

When I Complete My Shot ..... I'm Moving On, And I Know Where I'm Going

When I Finish A Hole .... The Green Belongs To The Next Group

When I'm Watching You Hit ... I'm Positioned Where I'm Supposed To Be

When I Lay Down My Clubs ... They Are On The Path To My Next Destination

When I'm In The Bunker ...... The Rake Is There With Me

When I Park My Cart .... I'm Not Coming Back For More Clubs

When I'm On The Tee/Green ... I Know When It's My Turn

When I'm Playing My Shot ..... My Routines Are Simple

When I'm On The Course ...... I'm Keeping Up Or Moving Aside

When I Play Golf .... I Play Four Under **Golf!**

SECTION THREE

THE GREATEST GAME OF ALL

Keeping Golf in Good Hands -

Ours

LIGHTS ... CAMERA ... ACTION!

It's game time and you're on the tee!

<u>THE RETURN of the FOUR HOUR ROUND</u> was not created for you to read, place beside you on the couch and mutter – *"That was very interesting. I sure hope that slow play problem gets sorted out. Darling, do you want to watch American Idol tonight?"*

I realize that I neglected to inform you that you had an *active* role to play in this entire movement. Sorry about that! Think of it as if you went to the doctor and he informed you that the solution to your problem was simple. He notes that if you drink two glasses of water per day your problem will go away. He's given you the solution. However, the solution is useless unless you drink the water.

The same applies to the issue of Global Slowing in golf. We understand the problem. We have identified the solution however:

The solution to a problem is only successful when combined with action.

The objective of Four Under Golf is not simply to identify the problem and define the solution. The objective is to RESOLVE the problem, and ultimately to ELIMINATE slow play from our golfing vocabulary. This is the definitive goal of Four Under Golf.

So, get off the couch. *American Idol* can wait. It's time for action. If we don't act, we've got no business EVER complaining about slow play again! It's time to be part of the solution.

*I see what's wrong, so now it's time
for me to get things going.*

*I can't stand by. I need to act
to help stop Global Slowing.*

REVERSING GLOBAL SLOWING
THE GOLFER'S TO-DO LIST!

"What can I do? After all, I'm just one person." Well, you may just be one person, but your influence is important. Your support is crucial. To stop the spread of Global Slowing in golf, we all need to take action, and make changes. It is not "someone else's problem" – it's OUR problem, and we're in it together. Together we can improve the state of the game. Following the four steps outlined below will help to reintroduce <u>THE RETURN of the FOUR HOUR ROUND!</u>

STEP #1
IMPROVE YOUR OWN HABITS

There are far too many golfers who feel that they have no personal role in the slow play issue. They understand it is a big problem, but they don't feel part of it. *"I play fine. It's not my problem. Get those other golfers to speed up!"* The reality is we all play a personal role in this issue.

Golf has been slowing for decades now. Fast players play slower than they used to, as do average and slow players. We ALL play at a slower pace, and ALL of us can improve our habits.

I play with golfers of all ages and abilities each year. The group I play with most often features golfers who play in less than four hours on a regular basis. There is one player in our group who always walks, plays at an excellent pace, but has one bad habit. He usually leaves his bag in the wrong position near the green. He rarely sets down his bag in the direction to the next tee, which requires him to waste time during its retrieval.

This habit is generally overlooked because Steve's other habits on the golf course are impeccable. He's always ready, and never out of position. He moves with purpose, and his routines are simple and efficient. The reason for Steve to change this behavior was simple; we all learn by example. We all set examples. The sooner bad habits are eliminated from the game, the quicker beneficial habits will take over!

The reality is that EVERYONE needs to improve his or her habits. **Make it your goal to improve at least one of your golfing habits** and begin this with your next round! After you have successfully integrated this improved behavior into your golf game, continue the improvement process with another habit.

STEP #2
SET AN EXAMPLE

We are all role models. It's up to us whether we are good or bad models, but people learn from example. No matter what your ability level, if you play Four Under Golf, golfers will notice. They will see the benefits, and they will change their own habits for the better!

Step #2 is a fundamental responsibility for the golfing mentors of the world. This includes all golf professionals (touring and teaching), coaches, club champions, team leaders, parents, and grandparents. No matter what your level of golf, chances are somebody's looking at you as an example. Be a great example!

STEP #3
IT'S TIME TO SPEAK UP

Confronting other players can be difficult. However, this needs to be done. It does not, however, need to be uncomfortable or negative in nature. If a player steps in your line when you're putting, it's perfectly acceptable to mention this – *"Bill, excuse me, but you're standing in my line."* Bill accepts this, apologizes and learns from the experience.

It is time that golfers begin to speak with fellow golfers in terms of other "poor habits." It is the simplest way to improve the game for everyone.

Here are some simple examples:

Tom leaves a wedge at the front of the green following his chip shot: You pick up his wedge for him as he's putting.

"Tom, I got your wedge. It's over there on the way to your golf cart." This is a great start in pointing out that he SHOULD HAVE done this on his own. If Tom is chronically negligent when it comes to this behavior, it may be time to add: *"The best thing to do, Tom, is to pick up your extra clubs following your chip and place them over here where Bill and Steve placed their clubs. It's on the way to the cart, so you don't have to go out of your way when you finish the hole. This would help speed up play, and you've got less chance of leaving a club behind."*

Tom (poor Tom has some bad habits!) hits his bunker shot without taking the rake into the bunker with him: You toss him the rake. *"Tom, here's the rake. You are allowed to bring the rake in with you. I'm not sure if you know this, but it's not against the rules."* This is a great reminder to Tom as to what he SHOULD DO. Again, if this is a regular problem you may wish to add: *"In fact, Tom, taking the rake in with you virtually cuts your movements in half. It's now your turn to putt and if you had to go out, get the rake, go back into the bunker to complete your raking – well, you can see that's a serious waste of time."*

There are obviously countless situations where gentle, but direct, confrontation can be beneficial. Litter was highly visible years ago. Only when it became socially unacceptable did the problem dissipate. Whereas a person 50 years ago may have simply thrown his candy wrapper out the window of the car, that person would be confronted today. *"Johnny, do NOT throw that wrapper out the window!"* Golfers have adapted unacceptable behaviors that need to be identified and eliminated. Nothing is going to change if Johnny keeps throwing the wrapper out of the window. And, he's probably not going to stop until someone says something to him!

It's time for golfers to take responsibility for their behaviors, and to draw attention to actions that are detrimental to the game. We will have made monumental strides when we hear the following commentary during a golf telecast: *"Bill's got a tricky ten-footer to save par. What the heck is Fabio doing over there? He's got a four-footer coming up next and he's 40 feet from nowhere talking to his caddy about the weather. My goodness, that's a terrible example to set for golfers around the world watching this telecast."*

STEP #4
SPREAD THE WORD

Four Under Golf will be as successful as we, the golfers of the world, make it. Understanding the solution is not enough. This movement must spread like a great joke on the Internet. Now that you know the punch line, it's your job to keep it moving.

The symbol of Four Under Golf was designed for a reason. A **red 4** is the universal symbol for four-under par. It is featured on all of the championship leader boards throughout the world, and generally a score worth striving for. The **red -4** is the symbol for Four Under Golf. Four-under par is a great goal, attainable for only a fraction of the golfing world. Four Under Golf is a responsibility we all share, and attainable for every golfer.

We may not all shoot four-under par, but we can play Four Under Golf!

The final item on your to-do list: Spread the word - and start becoming a part of the solution.

My to-do list is very clear
and my enthusiasm abounds.

To aid the cause for THE RETURN
of the FOUR HOUR ROUND!

WHY SHOULD I "JUST HIT IT"?

There's a great question. *Why should I just hit it?* I understand that it would be great for the game if golf were played at a better pace. But, what does it do for me and my game?

Golf is unique in that it is not only a large spectator sport; it also has a high participation level in all age groups. Most 50-year-old individuals are not putting on the shoulder pads each weekend for a football scrimmage, or going to the diamond for batting practice. Golfers of all ages watch the pros play on the weekend, then hit the links to participate at their own personal level. There are positives and negatives to this unique relationship.

The positive side is enormous. It provides great entertainment. Golfers can actually play the same courses as their idols. The fact that we play the game allows us to more readily relate to the successes and failures of the greatest players. Observing great golf can be extremely inspirational.

A negative side of this relationship is an area that has grown as more fame, fortune, and exposure is placed in the hands of those chasing the treasures. The televised golfer has become an *entertainer*. The more time he or she is visible on television and in the public eye, the greater his or her endorsements and bank balances. Cameras follow the player as he walks around his putt (in slow motion), and analyzes his chances. *"This putt is important"* according to Mr. Commentator, and the movement of a golf ball from its current location into a four-and-a-half inch hole becomes an intense mental exercise. It also requires a physical motion that, according to Mr. Commentator, all of the viewers *"would do themselves well to observe and copy."*

The incredible slowing of the game on the professional level may or may not have had a major effect on viewership of golf in general. That's another discussion. It has, however, had a profound negative effect on the pace of play throughout the game as a whole. It is beginning to snowball, as golfers are leaving the game and prospective new golfers aren't gravitating to the game because *"it takes too long, and it's a constant stop-and-go."*

An additional negative is that this Global Slowing of the game isn't making any of us any better! Should you "JUST HIT IT?" Golf is unique, but it is still a sport. Let's look at a few nuances you may find interesting:

Does taking your time help you play better? Now, there's a question worth considering.

Because the golf ball is stationary, and we don't set specific time limits to hit golf shots, golf presents an unusual challenge. In most sports, reaction is a key ingredient. In tennis, the ball is hit toward you, requiring you to react and hit it back. The baseball is pitched, so you swing. In other words, something triggers your movements. That is not the case in golf.

Other sports have time limits, which create much of the excitement. You have the 24-second clock in basketball, 15-minute quarters in football, timed periods in hockey, etc. Time parameters play important roles in instigating activities in each of these sports.

Golf is a sport that places a player's responsibility on a higher plane. There have always been rules to play by, but the dignity of the game has always been placed on the shoulders of the golfer. Thus, such issues as time limits were seldom instituted, because a golfer would never consider playing at a pace that detracted from the enjoyment of others. Ah, the good ol' days.

Does all of this *free time* to plan, figure, and calculate help us perform better? Answer this question:

There are two seconds to go in the Super Bowl between New York and Seattle. New York lines up to kick a potential game-winning field goal. Seattle calls time out. Why would Seattle call time out?

Well, if you're a sports fan or you've competed in any sporting activity you know why. Even the commentators will note: *"They want to give Paul Placekicker a little more time to think about this one."* Well, wouldn't more time to think about it and plan out his kick be a good thing for the kicker?

Nope – you know what the kicker wants to do - Just Kick It!

Golf is the only sport in the world where we call time out on ourselves!

There are thousands of correlations you can examine, from shooting free throws, to throwing passes to covered receivers, but the bottom line is this: Practice, train, and prepare to your heart's desire. When you get on the course to play the game – JUST HIT IT! Will you play better and enjoy it more – absolutely! Does this mean you're not trying? Not at all! Isn't Kobe Bryant still trying even when he only dribbles once before shooting a free throw?

Spending more time does not mean you're trying better. You may argue that you're trying harder, but that's a far cry from trying better. Unfortunately, the 21st Century golfer doesn't always understand this. Great dancers dance. Ballplayers shoot, throw, and catch. The modern golfer often stands around and analyzes, and believes the harder he *tries* on each shot, the better he'll do. In far too many cases, he doesn't "play golf" anymore.

There is a prevailing notion among golfers that spending more time will help them with concentration and focus. Somehow due to time-consuming mental preparation their shots will improve, and their scores will lower. I'm not sure which genius first implanted this into the brain of the modern golfer, but it's time for a mass lobotomy!

Concentration and focus are vital attributes in all sports. If there is a correlation between time spent *thinking* prior to the performance of the physical act, and success, the modern golfer passes that moment of maximum benefit about the time he finally takes a club out of his bag!

Go to a local English pub, grab a dart and attempt to hit the center circle. Are you concentrating? Are you focused? Have you ever seen a great dart thrower stand and "practice throw," or take obscene amounts of time to throw the dart?

The reality is that concentration and focus do not necessarily improve because extra time is utilized in the process. The modern golfer is generally more concerned about maintaining the appearance of trying hard than he is about actually playing golf. He stands around and tries to "out try" his fellow golfers, extending his preparation time to new outrageous heights. The process, of course, has no positive effect on his golf game, increases his anxiety, decreases the enjoyment of his playing partners, and slows the entire game for everyone on the course. *Global Slowing continues…*

Golf is a game of motion, filled with great challenges that inspire us. The ball flying through the air, bouncing, spinning and rolling is exhilarating to witness. Golf can be a source of great joy, blessed with a unique combination of competition and sociability.

We need to stop the slowing. Teachers need to teach this every day. At the end of the day, this is much more important than the proper pre-shot routine. It's time for a return to sanity!

Four Under Golf is a symbol for something we should all care about as we pass the game on to the next generation. It's the greatest game of all, and it's OURS. Let's all be part of the solution, and JUST HIT IT!

It's our great game that brings us joy,
so let's never regret it.

Dancers dance and pitchers pitch,
true golfers, they just hit it!

THAT WHICH CONTINUALLY SLOWS NEEDS TO CHANGE HOW IT FLOWS!

A NEW BEGINNING

The beginning of the 21st Century saw golf slowing to unprecedented levels. The current golf season began with the final groups during televised professional tournaments taking up to five-and-a-half hours to complete their rounds. Golf participation was continuing to fall, and golf courses were struggling to make ends meet. *"These guys are good"* could easily have been changed to *"These guys are slow"* as the slogan for the PGA Tour. The game of golf was slowing to a crawl.

What comes next? Let's come together to make this happen...

Suddenly a great shift occurred, and the slowing of the game began to subside. Golfers started to take responsibility for their actions, and behaviors began to improve. Teachers worked to incorporate the teaching of positive habits. Touring professionals accepted the challenge to improve their golfing behaviors, and the pace of play improved during their events. This led to more entertaining telecasts, and increased viewership. The golfing public, from beginners to professionals, started to rally together for the good of the game.

Golf continued to prosper. The years that followed saw steady growth in all areas of the game. People started to gravitate to the course again. Club memberships increased, as did play at public and resort courses. Tournament entries increased, as did the enjoyment level associated with participation. As the pace of play continued to improve, all aspects of the game flourished.

Yes, the Golden Era of Golf began when the Age of Global Slowing came to an end. Golf historian *NineUnder Nick* notes – *"It appears that there was a dramatic shift in the behaviors golfers employed near the beginning of the 21st Century. We speculate that a giant wake-up call of sorts occurred, leading to a reversal in a slowing trend that lasted nearly 50 years. We should all be thankful, because the game as we know it may not exist today if the Age of Global Slowing was allowed to continue."*

Thank you golfers, young and old
we're truly glad you found.

That 18 holes are simply played
in a four hour round.

ARE YOU A FOUR UNDER GOLFER?

THE FOUR UNDER GOLF TEST

Take the test on the following pages, and give it to your friends and golfing companions. Your answers represent your golfing behaviors. Changing behaviors can be easily accomplished. However, this requires awareness. Watch your fellow golfers during your next round, and you'll see clearly how the pace of play is affected by our behaviors.

Preparation – The 1st Tee:

1) Do you arrive to the first tee at least five minutes prior to your tee time?
Yes_____ No_____

2) When it is your turn to tee off on hole #1, have you completed the following?

   a) Marked your ball with identifying mark?
   Yes_____ No_____

   b) Counted your clubs? Yes_____ No_____

   c) Secured tees and ball markers?
   Yes_____ No_____

   d) Secured necessary items for the day?
   (clothing/umbrellas/golf balls, gloves, etc)
   Yes _____ No_____

   e) Made necessary introductions and confirmed the competition for the round?
   Yes_____ No_____

   f) Completed necessary practice/loosening up and preparation? Yes_____ No_____

   g) Pulled your club from the bag and are ready to hit?
   Yes_____ No_____

3) Do you have a marked provisional ball, either in your pocket or easy to reach? Yes_____ No_____

Four Under Golfers answered YES
to all of the above.

Teeing Area Behaviors:

1) When do you write down scores?

   a) On the previous green ___

   b) On the tee, prior to teeing off ___

   c) Following completion of the hole, but never at a time that delays our group or the group following us ___

2) When I walk onto the tee (playing in a cart):

   a) I check out the hole – return to the cart for a club ___

   b) I sit in the cart writing scores or relaxing until it's my turn to hit ___

   c) I take the club(s) I may need to the tee, even if this is a multiple group of clubs ___

3) When it's my turn to tee off:

   a) I wait until the player before me hits; I make my decisions, check the elements, (wind, lie, slope, etc.) find a nice teeing area, start my preparations, and then play my shot ___

   b) I often don't know when it's my turn, so I wait until someone tells me, or I ask – "Am I up?" ___

   c) I move into the teeing area without delay, prepared to play ___

4) When I've completed my tee shot:

   a) I watch the shot until the ball stops, not moving from my space until I'm ready ____

   b) I stand on the tee following my shots, commenting on my swing, and perhaps taking a couple more swings to get it "grooved" ____

   c) After hitting my shot, satisfied there's no danger of the ball being lost or in trouble, I pick up my tee and move immediately from the teeing area allowing the following player to hit ____

5) After I've hit my shot and moved from the tee:

   a) I stand and take some practice swings or look around at the scenery ____

   b) I talk about my shot, or tell a story to my playing partners ____

   c) I find the location out of the way/view of the next player, and in the nearest proximity to my golf bag/golf cart which still allows me to view the next player's shot. If easily managed, I will also put my club in the bag at this time ____

Four Under Golfers answered "C"
to all of the above.

Around The Course:

1) Walkers. When I'm walking the course:

    a) I go to my playing partner's ball, watch him hit, and then move on to my ball ____

    b) I move to my ball directly, taking the simplest line without disturbing the play of any other golfer in my group ____

2) Riders. When my cart partner and I get to the first ball to play (which is his):

    a) I wait for him to complete play, and then we drive to my ball ____

    b) If circumstances permit, I will either drop my partner off with ample clubs and move towards my ball, or I will take ample clubs and walk to my ball while he is preparing to play ____

3) When the player hitting before me is playing/preparing to play:

    a) I wait for the player to hit then begin to move toward my ball. I begin my preparation when I arrive at my ball ____

    b) I am in a position that does not disturb his preparation or play, and allows me the easiest access to move into my shot without delay ____

4) When I hit a wayward shot:

   a) I go to look for my ball first. If I don't find it, I'll go back and hit another ball ___

   b) I hit a provisional ball ___

5) A player in my group hits a ball into a position where a search is required:

   a) Everyone in the group goes in search of the ball until it is found or the player abandons the ball ___

   b) Players in our group nearest to his ball will assist, the other players will alternate between searching for the ball and playing their own shots ___

6) Our group has a hole open in front of us, and the group behind us is waiting on us regularly:

   a) We're only a hole behind, so it's not an issue ___

   b) We move aside, allowing the faster group to pass ___

   c) We're playing at an acceptable pace, there's no issue ___

   d) We'll just try and play faster ___

   e) I never notice what other groups are doing ___

Four Under Golfers answered "B"
to all of the above.

In The Bunker:

1) I've hit the ball into the bunker:

    a) I walk into the bunker and hit my shot. I then depart the bunker; find the rake and return to rake the bunker ___

    b) I walk into the bunker with the rake. I hit my shot and rake the trap, departing in the same line as my entry ___

2) I've hit the ball into the bunker:

    a) I walk into the bunker at the closest edge in relation to my ball, regardless of the slope ___

    b) I walk into the bunker at the location that is the safest, allows the simplest situation for raking, and provides the easiest exit ___

3) I've hit the ball into the greenside bunker:

    a) I will hit my bunker shot, then return to the cart, or my bag, and get my putter ___

    b) I have my putter with me, and I've placed it in a location where I won't miss it when I depart the bunker ___

Four Under Golfers answered "B"
to all of the above.

Finally On The Green:

1) Walkers. When I arrive onto the green:

    a) I put my bag down near my ball, without setting it on the green ____

    b) I set my bag in a location that allows me the straightest line between the flag and the next teeing area ____

    c) I don't really think about where I set my bag ____

2) Riders. When I arrive onto the green:

    a) I leave the cart in any position; it's either on the path, or away from the green ____

    b) I leave the cart in a position that allows me to get to the green easily, following course rules, and not causing course damage. The cart is located so that my walk back to the cart will not cause excessive delay for the players behind me ____

3) I sometimes arrive at the green with extra clubs (in addition to my putter):

    a) I set these in an area around where I'm putting, or where I hit my previous chip or approach ____

    b) I place these in a visible area that is in a direct line from the hole to either my cart or my golf bag, and not in the way of any other player ____

4) There is one player left to putt-out in our group:

   a) I stand and watch him putt out, then I move to get my spare clubs, grabbing the pin if necessary ____

   b) I'm either holding the pin, ready to place it in the hole following completion – or I'm standing in an area – not in the players view and is "on the way" to either my golf bag or golf cart. I have my spare clubs in my hands ____

5) A player is just about to putt, and I'm next in the putting order:

   a) I'm watching him putt, staying out of his line of sight ____

   b) I'm courteous to my playing partner, staying out of his line, but I've also chosen a position to stand that is as close to my ball as I can get (without disturbance to the player putting) ____

6) It is now my turn to putt:

   a) I place my ball down in its location. I then begin lining up my putt ____

   b) I place my ball down. I have done as much "lining up" as possible prior to my turn to putt ____

7) I've hit my first putt, and it finishes several feet from the hole:

   a) I'm not happy. I stand in my current spot, complain a little, take a few practice strokes, and meander up to my ball. I then mark my ball ___

   b) I'm not happy, I move directly to my ball and either mark it immediately, or putt my next putt into the hole ___

Four Under Golfers answered "B"
to all of the above.

We All Have Routines:

1) Once I'm in my set up position:

   a) I stand over the ball in this position for an extended time ___

   b) I swing the club ___

2) After I've hit my shot:

   a) I often stand and try to figure out what I did right or wrong. I'll take a couple extra swings, maybe comment to those around me. When I'm through with my post-shot antics, I'll move on ___

   b) I watch where the ball goes, fix my divot, return my club to the bag, and move on ___

3) On the putting green:

   a) I look at each putt from all possible angles. I get down in a crouched position to really "see" the line. I plumb-bob, and fix every possible mark in my line, no matter how insignificant ___

   b) I do much of my "lining up" prior to my turn. My line-up is simple – I do not cause undue delay in the process ___

Four Under Golfers answered "B"
to all of the above.

Additional Routine Items To Consider:

4) It's my turn to putt, and I've done my "lining up." From this point, on a standard putt, my routine of practice strokes (and any other pre-putt antics) will take:

a) Less than 5 seconds to putt ____

b) Between 5 and 10 seconds to putt ____

c) Between 10 and 20 seconds to putt ____

d) Between 20 and 30 seconds to putt ____

e) Over 30 seconds to putt____

f) I have no idea how long it takes me to hit my putt ____

5) When the tee is clear and it's my turn to hit, on average it takes me:

a) Less than 15 seconds to hit my shot and clear the tee ____

b) Between 15 and 30 seconds to hit my shot and clear the tee ____

c) Between 30 and 60 seconds to hit my shot and clear the tee ____

d) Over a minute to hit my shot and clear the tee ____

e) I have no idea how long it takes me ____

6) My routine prior to hitting full shots includes:

a) Practice swings:

0 _____ 1 _____ 2 _____ 3 _____ 4+_____

b) Throwing grass in the air _____

c) Waggles: 0 _____ 1 -3 _____ multiple _____

d) Consultation with other player(s) _____

e) Using yardage device _____

f) Pacing yardage _____ or estimating yardage based on visible markers _____

g) Extensive time in selection of club _____

h) Often "backing away" from shots after set up _____

Working to decrease the time taken to complete the above is a responsibility we all share.

Even though I'm not a pro
I still can't help but wonder.

Why all of us, right from the start
weren't taught to play Four Under

UNTIL NOW!

QUICK CHECK SUMMARY

PLAYING FOUR UNDER GOLF UTILIZING THE 4 HABITS OF THE FOUR UNDER GOLFER

ON THE TEE - FROM TEE TO GREEN - ON THE GREEN

<u>ON THE TEE</u>

Be Prepared

1) **Know when it's your turn to tee off.** Be aware of your position in the hitting order.

2) **Secure all necessary items in advance.** This includes having your ball marked, tees in your pocket, and your club picked out. Do not let keeping score delay your tee shot.

3) **Avoid return trips to your cart or bag.** Take multiple clubs with you when applicable.

Be In Position

1) **Your 'on-deck-circle':** Find the nearest spot to your tee without being in the sight line of the person hitting.

2) **When you have completed your tee shot, move to your bag or in a position nearest your cart.** Replace your club at this time if this does not disturb the play of others.

Move With Purpose

1) **Move immediately to the tee when it's your turn to hit.**

2) **Move away from the tee when you have completed your shot**. The tee box is on loan to you. You don't OWN it.

3) **No unnecessary delays:** There are times to tell stories, and times to hit your shot. When it's your turn to hit, and the hole is open – that is NOT a time to tell stories!

Simplify Your Routines

1) **Know what you're going to do before you get to the tee**. Preparation assists with your routines. Understand your objective and perform your shot without undue delay.

2) **Throw out the garbage.** You need to tee up the ball, and hit the ball. All other activities make up your "routine". Focus on what is important and 'throw away' the rest of the unnecessary and non-productive activities.

3) **To simplify your routines, you need to practice them**. Practice these on the driving range, and take these (simple) routines to the course. This includes practice swings (0 to 1), lining up your shot, waggles or pre-shot movements, standing over the ball, and post shot movements. None of these require much time, and doing these simply and efficiently will help your game (and everyone's game).

PLAYING FOUR UNDER GOLF UTILIZING THE 4 HABITS OF THE FOUR UNDER GOLFER

FROM TEE TO GREEN

Be Prepared

1) **Begin planning your shot in advance.** Obtain the information you require to hit your next shot as you approach your ball.

2) **It's OK to prepare while others are playing**. Your preparation must not, of course, disturb play. But, in most cases you are easily able to begin preparing for your shot while others continue with their game.

Be In Position

1) **Always be in position to move to your ball, without disturbing play, in the simplest manner.** ie... The nearest point.

2) **If you are sharing a cart, drop off your playing partner and move to your shot whenever possible.** Or, leave your playing partner with the cart and walk to your ball (with your clubs in hand!).

3) **Do not move from player A, to player B, to player C in "packs".** It is fine to watch others play, but do not let it be a detriment to moving to your ball in the most efficient manner.

Move With Purpose

1) **Your purpose is to move to your ball in order to hit your next shot**. This can be accomplished while carrying on conversations, whistling, or daydreaming. However, do not lose track of what you are doing. You are participating in an activity that requires your attention and you have a responsibility to perform your tasks without excessive delay.

2) **Know where you are going next**. Think ahead and plan your movements with this in mind.

3) **Take the rake into the bunker with you**. Minimize your movements when possible.

Simplify Your Routines

1) **Routines include preparation items – don't wait to prepare**. Preparation includes getting yardages, throwing grass in the air, fiddling with your clubs, deep breathing, and countless other items that golfers go through (and don't go through). The simpler you make these, the more focus you will have towards actually playing golf.

2) **There are two things to do:** Picking a club, and hitting the ball. Simplifying your routines will help return you to the core of the game's objective.

PLAYING FOUR UNDER GOLF UTILIZING THE 4 HABITS OF THE FOUR UNDER GOLFER

ON THE GREEN

Be Prepared

1) **Preparation for your putt begins when you arrive on the green**. It does not begin "when it's your turn to putt".

2) **Check your line, speed, and contour of the green before it's your turn to putt**. This can and should be done while those before you "line-up" their putts. This can be easily accomplished without disturbing the play of others.

3) **Preparation makes you "ready".** When you prepare properly, the putting process will simply include placing your ball down and putting it into the hole (and with more success!).

Be In Position

1) **Remember the 'on-deck-circle'.** Position yourself in a nearby position so that you can move directly to your ball when it's your turn – without delay.

2) **Position all of your items properly (bag, towels, extra clubs, etc...).** Locate where you are moving to next (either your cart or the next tee). Position your items in a direct line to that location - and in clear sight.

3) **Know how to depart the green.** When you have completed your putting, either retrieve the pin and be prepared to replace it following play – or – be in a position that does not disturb play, and is in the direction of where you are going next.

Move With Purpose

1) **Know the positions of all the balls on the green**. Move into your position without delay so that when it's your turn to putt, you are ready to putt.

2) **Depart the green understanding that it now belongs to the next group**.

Simplify Your Routines

1) **Take your 'putting-game' from practice to the course.** Develop a simple routine on the putting green and stick to it on the course.

2) **Preparation is part of your routine.** Do as much as possible prior to your putt.

3) **Think "free throws".** More time does not necessarily equate to better results. It only equates to more time (for everyone).

4) **What are you looking at?** Don't fall into the trap of spending ages looking from all sides, and attempting to 'analyze' every minute detail of the putt. Do you do this because you've seen others do it, or is this truly a great benefit to your putting? Is all that time you spend wandering around helping you, or is it simply part of your routine? There is only one thing it is definitely doing – slowing the game!

About The Author

Pat Mateer was born in 1954 in Whittier, California. Pat's father introduced him to the game of golf at the age of 10. It has been a major part of his life since then.

Mateer participated in junior, high school, and college golf. He played professionally between 1977 and 1985. During this period, he traveled throughout the world, participating on various international tours. Retaining his amateur status in 1987, Mateer continues to participate in amateur events on the local and national level.

Golf also dominates the business life of Mateer. Mateer founded Championship Golf, Inc. in 1986, and continues to serve as President. Championship Golf operates golf events throughout the world.

For more information about Championship Golf, go to www.championshipgolftournaments.com.

Pat lives in Mission Viejo, California with his wife, Karen. He's a member at El Niguel Country Club and the Spyglass Hill Founder's Club.

Pat Mateer is a Four Under Golfer.

Acknowledgments

The idea for this book started in 1990. I apologize for the delay, but I got behind some slow groups! Actually, work and life sometimes require us to take detours. Since golf has continued to slow over the past twenty years, and with no change in sight, I decided it was time to focus on this project before it was too late. Needless to say, I had great support and enlightening insight from many people during this process.

Thanks to all of my friends who read through proofs, listened to my ideas, and showed great support. Special thanks to John Castle, Chuck Gall, and Steve Cook - lifelong friends and golf partners who helped to keep me focused. Mark King helped direct my energies, giving me alternative perspectives that shaped key areas of the project. Linda Maddox was a wealth of information and support during the production stages. Roseanne Brown was the creative brain that took my words, thoughts, and ideas and turned them into this book. Finally to my wife, Karen – thank you for your constant inspiration and encouragement every day.